baby einstein

Poetry

The WALT DISNEY Company

D0344963

Poetry Credits:
"Spring Rain" and "Going to Bed" by Marchette Chute (1909–1994). From *Around and About* by Marchette Chute. Copyright © 1957 by E.P. Dutton. Copyright renewed 1985 by Marchette Chute. Reprinted by permission of Elizabeth Hauser • "Animal Crackers" by Christopher Morley (1890–1957) • "Furry Bear" by A.A. Milne (1882–1956). From *When We Were Very Young* by A.A. Milne, illustrated by E.H.Shepard, copyright © 1924 by E.P. Dutton, renewed © 1952 by A.A. Milne. Used by permission of Dutton's Children's Books, a division of Penguin Young Readers Group, a member of Penguin Group (USA) Inc., 345 Hudson St., New York, NY 10014. All rights reserved • "Jack Frost" by Laura E. Richards (1850–1943) • "Caterpillars" by Aileen Fisher (1906–2002). From *Crickets in a Thicket* by Aileen Fisher, copyright © 1963 Aileen Fisher. Reprinted by permission of Marian Reiner on behalf of the Boulder Public Library Foundation. All rights reserved • "Goodnight" by Rose Fyleman. Permission by the Society of Authors as the Literary Representative of the Estate of Rose Fyleman.

Hyperion Books for Children, New York
For information address Hyperion Books for Children, 114 Fifth Avenue, New York, New York 10011-5690.
Printed in China
Library of Congress Cataloging Card Number on file.
ISBN 0-7868-3802-7

Visit www.hyperionbooksforchildren.com and www.babyeinstein.com

Great Minds Start Little.™

Singing

Of speckled eggs the birdie sings
And nests among the trees;
The sailor sings of ropes and things
In ships upon the seas.

The children sing in far Japan,
The children sing in Spain;
The organ with the organ man
Is singing in the rain.

Spring Rain
Marchette Chute

The storm came up so very quick
It couldn't have been quicker.
I should have brought my hat along,
I should have brought my slicker.

My hair is wet, my feet are wet,
I couldn't be much wetter.
I fell into a river once
But this is even better.

Who Likes the Rain
Clara Doty Bates

"I," said the duck, "I call it fun,
For I have my little red rubbers on;
They make a cunning three-toed track
In the soft, cool mud. Quack! Quack! Quack!"

"I" cried the dandelion, "I.
My roots are thirsty, my buds are dry"
And she lifted a tousled yellow head
Out of her green and grassy bed.

"I hope 'twill pour! I hope 'twill pour!"
Purred the tree toad at his gray back door,
"For, with a broad leaf for a roof,
I'm perfectly weather-proof."

"I" sang the brook: "I laugh at every drop,
And wish they never need to stop
Till a big, big river I grew to be,
And could find my way out to the sea."

"I" shouted Ted, "for I can run,
With my high-top boots and my raincoat on,
Through every puddle and runlet and pool
That I find on my way to school."

Mix a Pancake
Christina Rossetti

Mix a pancake,
Stir a pancake,
Pop it in the pan;
Fry the pancake,
Toss the pancake—
Catch it if you can.

Animal Crackers
Christopher Morley

Animal crackers, and cocoa to drink,
That is the finest of suppers, I think.
When I'm grown up and can have what I please,
I think I shall always insist upon these.

What do you choose when you're offered a treat?
When Mother says, "What would you like best to eat?"
Is it waffles and syrup, or cinnamon toast?
It's cocoa and animals that I love the most!

The kitchen's the coziest place that I know:
The kettle is singing, the stove is aglow,
And there in the twilight, how jolly to see
The cocoa and animals waiting for me.

The Swing

How do you like to go up in a swing;
Up in the air so blue?
Oh, I do think it the pleasantest thing
Ever a child can do!

Up in the air and over the wall;
Till I can see so wide,
Rivers and trees and cattle and all
Over the countryside—

Till I look down on the garden green,
Down on the roof so brown—
Up in the air I go flying again,
Up in the air and down!

Bed in Summer

In winter I get up at night
And dress by yellow candlelight.
In summer, quite the other way,
I have to go to bed by day.

I have to go to bed and see
The birds still hopping on the tree;
Or hear the grown-up people's feet
Still going past me in the street.

And does it not seem hard to you,
When all the sky is clear and blue,
And I should like so much to play,
To have to go to bed by day?

Furry Bear
A. A. Milne

If I were a bear,
And a big bear too,
I shouldn't much care
If it froze or snew;
I shouldn't much mind
If it snowed or friz—
I'd be all fur-lined
With a coat like his!

For I'd have fur boots and a brown fur wrap,
And brown fur knickers and a big fur cap.
I'd have a fur muffle-ruff to cover my jaws,
And brown fur mittens on my big brown paws.
With a big brown furry-down up to my head,
I'd sleep all the winter in a big fur bed.

Jack Frost
Laura E. Richards

Jack Frost, Jack Frost,
Came in the night;
He left the meadows that he crossed
All gleaming white.
Painted with his silver brush
Every windowpane;
Kissed the leaves and made them blush,
Blush and blush again.

Jack Frost, Jack Frost,
Crept around the house,
Sly as a silver fox,
Still as a mouse.
Out little Jenny came,
Blushing like a rose;
Up jumped Jack Frost,
And pinched her little nose.

The Plumpuppets
Christopher Morley

When little heads weary have gone to their beds,
When all the good nights and prayers have been said,
Of all the good fairies that send bairns to rest
The little Plumpuppets are those I love best.

If your pillow is lumpy, or hot, thin, and flat,
The little Plumpuppets know just what they're at:
They plump up the pillow, all soft, cool and fat....
The little Plumpuppets plump up it!

The little Plumpuppets are fairies of beds;
They have nothing to do but watch sleepyheads;
They turn down the sheets and they tuck you in tight,
And dance on your pillow to wish you good night!

No matter what troubles have bothered the day,
Though your doll broke her arm or the pup ran away;
Though your handies are black with ink that was spilt . . .
Plumpuppets are waiting in blanket and quilt.

If your pillow is lumpy, or hot, thin, and flat,
The little Plumpuppets know just what they're at:
They plump up the pillow, all soft, cool and fat . . .
The little Plumpuppets plump up it!

If You See a Faery Ring
William Shakespeare

If you see a faery ring
In a field of grass,
Very lightly step around,
Tip-toe as you pass,
Last night faeries frolicked there . . .
And they're sleeping somewhere near.
If you see a tiny faery,
Lying fast asleep
Shut your eyes
And run away,
Do not stay to peek!
Do not tell
Or you'll break a faery spell.

Where Go the Boats?

Dark brown is the river,
Golden is the sand.
It flows along forever,
With trees on either hand.

Green leaves a-floating,
Castles of the foam,
Boats of mine a-boating—
Where will all come home?

On goes the river
And out past the mill,
Away down the valley,
Away down the hill.

Away down the river,
A hundred miles or more,
Other little children
Shall bring my boats ashore.

Caterpillars
Aileen Fisher

What do caterpillars do?
Nothing much but chew and chew.
What do caterpillars know?
Nothing much but how to grow.
They just eat what by and by
Will make them be a butterfly.
But that is more than I can do,
However much I chew and chew.

Little Black Bug
Margaret Wise Brown

Little black bug,
Little black bug,
Where have you been?
I've been under the rug.
Said little black bug.
Bug-ug-ug-ug.

Little green fly,
Little green fly,
Where have you been?
I've been way up high,
Said little green fly.
Bzzzzzzzzzzzzzzz.

Little old mouse,
Little old mouse,
Where have you been?
I've been all through the house,
Said little old mouse.
Squeak-eak-eak-eak-eak.

Going to Bed
Marchette Chute

I'm always told to hurry up—
Which I'd be glad to do,
If there were not so many things
That need attending to.

But first I have to find my towel
Which fell behind the rack,
And when a pillow's thrown at me
I have to throw it back.

And then I have to get the things
I need in bed with me.
Like marbles and my birthday train
And Pete the chimpanzee.

I have to see my polliwog
Is safely in its pan,
And stand a minute on my head
To be quite sure I can.

I have to bounce upon my bed
To see if it will sink,
and then when I am covered up
I find I need a drink.

Goodnight
Rose Fyleman

The rabbits play no more,
The little birds are weary,
The buttercups are folded up—
Good night, good night, my dearie.

The children in the country,
The children in the city,
Go to their beds with nodding heads—
Good night, good night, my pretty.

The Moon

The moon has a face like the clock in the hall;
She shines on the thieves on the garden wall,
On streets and fields and harbor quays,
And birdies asleep in the forks of the trees.

The squalling cat and the squeaking mouse,
The howling dog by the door of the house,
The bat that lies in bed at noon,
All love to be out by the light of the moon.

But all of the things that belong to the day
Cuddle to sleep to be out of her way;
And flowers and children close their eyes
Till up in the morning the sun shall arise.